MY FIRST BOOK OF
QUESTIONS
& ANSWERS

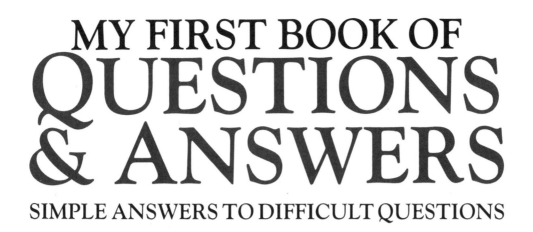

MY FIRST BOOK OF QUESTIONS & ANSWERS

SIMPLE ANSWERS TO DIFFICULT QUESTIONS

Written by Philip Steele
Illustrated by Kate Jaspers
Educational Adviser: Cliff Moon

DEAN

First published in 1989 by Hamlyn Books
This edition first published 1993 by
Dean, an imprint of Reed Consumer Books Ltd.,
Michelin House, 81 Fulham Road, London SW3 6RB

Copyright © 1989 Octopus Books Ltd.

Revised artwork for flags on pages 55 and 57
by Maltings Partnership

ISBN 0 603 55130 0

Produced by Mandarin Offset, printed in China

For Daniel and Edward, from Kate

Where to find out:

All about
food

Food

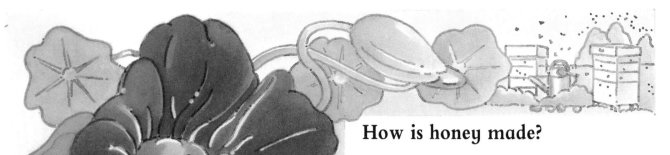

How is honey made?

Bees make honey from flowers.
Inside the petals of flowers there is
a sweet liquid called nectar.
Bees suck up nectar with
their tongues and then fly back to
their hive and give the nectar to
another bee.
This bee turns the nectar
into a food called honey
by chewing it in its mouth.
Bees store the honey in little wax
holes called cells.
Each of these cells has six sides.
Together the cells make up
a honeycomb.

Where does rice come from?

Rice is a plant which looks like
grass and it grows best in hot,
wet places.
Rice is grown in fields
which are flooded with water and
these are called paddy fields.
When the plants have grown
the fields are drained and the plants
are left to ripen in the sun.
Then people collect the plants and
thresh, or beat them to separate
the grains from the plants.
Rice can be eaten with meat or
vegetables or cooked in milk and
eaten as a pudding.
The Japanese use rice to
make a drink called saké.

What is chocolate made of?

Chocolate is made from
cocoa beans which grow
on the cacao tree.
This is a small tree which
grows in hot countries and
people grow it for its seeds,
which we call cocoa beans.
Cocoa beans are picked, roasted,
shelled and ground into powder.
This is mixed with milk and sugar or
other flavours to make chocolate.

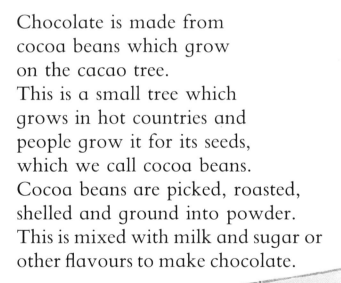

Food

Where does milk come from?

The milk most people drink
comes from cows.
Some animals feed their babies
with their mother's milk and
they are called mammals.
Humans are mammals and like to
drink the milk of some other
mammals – especially cows' milk.
Farmers milk their cows twice a
day using a special machine.
The milk is taken to a factory,
heated to kill off germs and
put into bottles or cartons.

What is butter made of?

Butter is made from milk.
Milk contains fat and water.
The fattiest part of the milk is
called cream and this is used
to make butter.
The cream is churned or shaken up.
This breaks the fat up into drops
and spreads them evenly
throughout the water.
Soon the drops stick together
and they harden into butter.

What is cheese made of?

Cheese is made from milk.
The milk is taken from mammals
such as cows, goats or sheep.
The milk is left in a warm place
to go sour or curdle.
After a time the milk separates
into solid lumps called curd and
a thin liquid called whey.
The whey is drained off and
the curd becomes cheese.

Food

What is bread made of?

Bread is made from crops, or plants such as wheat, rye, millet and corn or maize.
The grain from these plants can be ground down into a powder called flour.
Flour is mixed with water or milk to make bread.
Usually yeast is added to make the loaf rise up.
You can find out how this happens on the next page.
The baker bakes the loaf of bread in the oven.

What are cornflakes made of?

Cornflakes are flakes of corn.
Corn, or maize, is a tall plant which has cobs which are long yellow spikes full of grain.
The cobs are picked and taken to a factory where grains from the cob are steamed until they are soft.
Salt and sugar are added.
Then the soft grains are squashed flat by a big roller.
Finally they are toasted in an oven until they are crisp and then put into packets ready to be sold.

What is margarine made of?

Margarine is made from oils
mixed with water.
The oils are taken from vegetables
and seeds or from fish.
Usually oil and water
do not mix easily.
So the oil and water have to be
churned, or shaken until they are
well mixed together.
When this happens
the mixture becomes thick.
Sometimes milk is added to make
margarine taste like butter.

What is yeast?

Yeast is a fungus that is
yellow and gooey.
Yeast is used when you bake a cake
or a loaf of bread.
When yeast is wet it gives off gas.
This spreads through the mixture
and makes it rise up until it is light.

Food

Where does salt come from?

Salt can be found in rocks
and also in the sea.
People dig down to the rocks
which lie underground.
Then they wash all the salt out
with water.
The salt can then be dried out and
then it is ready to use.
Salt is also found in sea water.
In some places people take salt
from the sea.
They dig shallow ponds and
fill them with sea water.
As the sun shines it dries up
the water and piles of salt
are left behind.

Where does tea come from?

Tea comes from a type of bush
that grows in China, India,
Sri Lanka, Russia and parts
of Africa.
The smaller leaves are selected and
picked, rolled, dried and broken up.
By now the tea is dry and black.
The tea is packed in wooden chests
to be sent all over the world.
Later it is put in packets to be sold.

Where does sugar come from?

Sugar comes from plants but
it has to be specially treated
to turn it into the sort of sugar
you find in the shops.
Some sugar comes from a plant
called sugar cane.
This is a very tall plant
which looks like grass and
grows in hot countries.
The stalk of the cane is crushed.
This produces a juice
which is boiled until it is thick.
The crystals of sugar then form
from this thick mixture.
Sugar also comes from a plant
called sugar beet.
The sugar beet is sliced up and
the sweet juice is taken out.

Food

Why do oranges have pips?

Pips in an orange are really seeds
from which new trees can grow.
Fruit contains pips, seeds or stones.
When the fruit ripens on the tree
the seeds, stones or pips fall
to the ground or are blown away
by the wind.
Some of these seeds grow up into
a new tree which will have
fruit of its own.

Is fruit juice good for you?

Pure fruit juice tastes very nice.
It is also good for you because
it contains vitamin C.
This gives you healthy teeth and
bones and protects you from colds.
Vitamin C is found in oranges,
grapefruit, tomatoes and
green vegetables.

What are coconuts?

Coconuts are the seeds of the
coconut palm, a tree which grows
near the sea in hot countries.
It has a large green fruit and
inside the fruit there is a seed.
This is the hairy, brown coconut
you see in the shops.
Coconuts are often washed by
the sea from one shore to another
where they grow into new trees.

Food

Why is food frozen?

Food is frozen to keep it fresh.
There are tiny germs inside
all the food you eat.
They are called bacteria and
they can make food go rotten.
If food is kept very cold
bacteria cannot grow and spread.

Why is food put into cans?

Cans also keep food fresh.
Bacteria are the tiny germs in food
which can make it go bad and
they need air to grow.
One way to keep food fresh
is to put it in sealed cans
where no air can get in.
The food and cans must be clean
before the cans are filled.

What is curry?

Curry is a stew which is made
using different spices and herbs.
These spices and herbs make curry
taste very hot like pepper.
In hot countries food goes bad
if it is not kept cold.
Long ago people in hot countries
stopped their food going bad
by adding salt, pepper and spices.
And it tasted very good!
That is why people in hot countries
first ate spicy food like curry.
Today people all over the world
eat curry.

Food

Why is spaghetti long and thin?

Spaghetti is pasta which has been
pressed through a special machine
which turns it into long,
thin strands.
Pasta is made from flour and eggs
and can be made into all sorts
of shapes and sizes.
Spaghetti is the most wriggly food
in the world!
It was first made in Italy but
people say that the Italians
copied the idea from the Chinese.
Years ago an Italian explorer,
Marco Polo, visited China and
saw people eating noodles,
another sort of pasta.
He took the idea back
to his own country.

Food

Why is soup put into packets?

Soup is put into packets to
make it easier to store and so that
it can be kept for a long time.
If the water is taken out of food
like meat and vegetables it can
be dried and put into packets.
To make soup from a packet
you just add boiling water.
The water goes into the food and
makes it soft and ready to eat.

Why do people eat with chopsticks?

In some parts of the world
people use knives, forks and spoons
when they eat.
In other places people use
their hands to pick up their food.
They use chopsticks in China and
in many other countries in Asia.
Chopsticks are thin wooden rods.
Look how the girl in the picture
is holding hers.
They are between her thumb and
her first two fingers.
Eating with chopsticks may seem
difficult at first but it is easy
once you know how!

Food

How are potato crisps made?

People say the American Indians
first invented potato crisps
hundreds of years ago.
Today we make them like this:
potatoes are cut into thin slices
then fried in oil and dried.
Salt and all other kinds of
flavourings are often added too.

Are vegetables good for you?

Vegetables contain many things
that are good for you.
Some have vitamins to make you
grow strong, some contain iron
which is good for the blood.
Others contain calcium which
is good for your bones and teeth.
Many vegetables are made up
of rough fibre.
This helps food to pass
through your body.

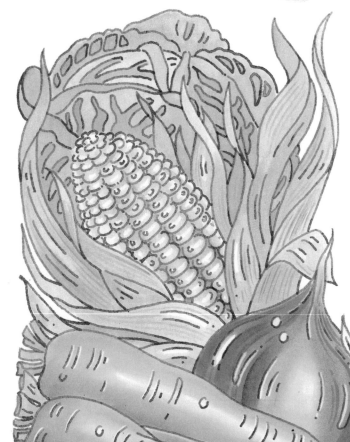

Food

Does it matter how much you eat?

If you eat too little you starve.
Your body soon becomes weak and
cannot fight off illnesses.
People who eat too much food
can become overweight.
To stay healthy you need to eat
the right amount of food and
take plenty of exercise.
The food you eat is a bit like
the fuel you put in a car.
It gives you the energy you need
every day.
As you walk or run
you use up your supply of fuel.

All about
nature

Nature

Why do trees have bark?

Trees have bark to protect them
from the heat, cold and damp.
Bark is the tough outside layer
of a tree.
It helps to keep out fungus and
some of the tiny insects which
can harm a tree.

How can you tell how old a tree is?

A tree trunk grows a new layer
of wood each year.
For every year there is one ring.
Count the rings and you will know
how old the tree is.
If a tree has enough water and
plenty of room to grow it makes
a thick layer of wood.
If not it will only grow a thin one.
If you look at a log
you can see these layers.
They spread out from the centre
in rings.
There are some trees alive today,
called bristlecone pines,
that are over 4000 years old.
That's as long ago as when
the ancient Egyptians were alive!

Why do trees go bare in winter?

Trees lose their leaves in winter
because there is less sunlight
during the cold winter months.
A tree uses its leaves to make food
for itself.
To do this it needs sunlight.
Towards the end of the year
the green colouring disappears and
the leaves turn red, brown or yellow.
The leaves soon die and
are blown away by the wind.
The branches look bare in winter
but if you look carefully
you will see new leaf buds
ready for the spring.
Not all trees go bare in winter.
Some trees keep their green leaves
all the year round and
they are called evergreens.

How tall can trees grow?

The tallest tree ever measured
was a Douglas Fir that grew
in Canada.
It was measured in 1902 and
it was 126 m (415 ft) tall:
as high as a ten-storey building!

Nature

Why is grass green?

The stems and leaves of grass and
most other plants are green because
they have a green colouring inside.
This colouring is very important
because it helps to make food.
The colouring is called chlorophyll.
The chlorophyll in plants takes in
the energy of sunlight and stores it.
Plants also take in water
through their roots and stems.
They also breathe in air
through tiny holes in their leaves.
Plants use the energy from sunlight
to turn water and air into sugar.
This sugar gives plants strength
to grow.
Plants that are not green,
like mushrooms, cannot make food
and take it in from the soil.

Do plants eat?

Yes, most plants make their food
using water and air to make sugar.
They also take food from the soil.
There are a few plants that catch
insects in sticky hairs and then take
in their juice through their leaves.
One of these plants is the sundew
which grows in marshes in the
United Kingdom.
Another is the Venus's flytrap
which grows in the United States.

Can plants feel things?

Plants cannot feel things as
people and animals do because
they do not have brains.
When you touch something
messages go to your brain
to tell you what is going on.
If you fall over and hurt your knee
a message will go to your brain and
this message makes you feel pain.
Plants do not have brains
so when you pick them
they cannot feel pain.

Nature

Why do dandelions go fluffy?

Dandelions go fluffy to help them
spread their seeds.
After a dandelion has flowered
its head becomes covered
with white fluffy hairs.
There is a little seed on the end
of each tuft of hair.
The tufts are so light that
they blow away in the wind.
When they land, the seeds can
grow into new dandelion plants.

Why do some plants scratch and sting you?

Plants that scratch and sting you
are simply protecting themselves.
Stings and prickles make it harder
for them to be trampled down,
picked or eaten.
A nettle sting can be painful.
If you brush against a nettle,
hairs on the leaves break open and
drop a liquid on to your skin
which makes it hurt.
Other plants have spikes and thorns
which can scratch.

Why are flowers pretty?

Flowers have bright colours and markings to attract bees and other insects.
Bees and insects help to pollinate flowers so that they make new seeds or fruit.
Insects come to flowers for food and as they fly between flowers a yellow powder called pollen brushes off on their bodies.
Pollen is made by the male part of the flower called the stamen.
Soon the pollen falls off on to the female part of the flower which is called the pistil.
This grows into fruit and seeds.

Nature

Why do cats have whiskers?

The long, bristly whiskers around a cat's mouth help it to feel its way around.

If it needs to squeeze through a narrow gap, a cat uses its whiskers to find out whether it will fit. All pet cats have whiskers. So do wild cats, lions and tigers.

Why do dogs prick up their ears?

Dogs can hear sounds that we cannot hear and that is why they prick up their ears for what seems to be no reason. They have much better hearing than we do.

**Why do cats turn around
before they go to sleep?**

Cats turn around before they sleep
because this is what they do
in the wild.
When members of the cat family
live in the wild they often sleep
on grassy earth or piles of leaves.
Before they sleep they turn around
to press a hollow in the grass to
make themselves comfortable.
Pet cats do just the same thing.
They turn around even if they
are sleeping on a carpet or basket.

Nature

How do birds fly?

Birds have bodies that are made for
flying.
They are very light and
their feathers help them to glide
through the air.
When air flows over their wings
it lifts them up.
Birds in the air move forward
by flapping their wings.
Sometimes birds can glide along
without flapping their wings at all.
This is because they use air currents
to carry them along.
Hot air always rises and birds use
this air to soar high into the sky.
Some birds can hover in the air
as a helicopter does.
They flap their wings up and down
very fast.
The hummingbird can do this
up to 90 times a second!
Not all birds can fly, however.
Penguins and ostriches for example
cannot fly.

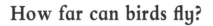

How far can birds fly?

The bird which flies the farthest
is the Arctic tern.
It spends half the year in the Arctic
and half in the Antarctic.
One tern found in Australia flew
over 22 500 km (14 000 miles)
from Russia – that's
half-way around the world!
Some birds spend the winter in one
part of the world and then fly off
to another land for the summer.
This is called migration.

How do chicks get out of their eggs?

When a chick is ready to hatch
it cracks open the shell of its egg
using its egg tooth.
The egg tooth is a little point
growing from the chick's beak.
When the baby bird is inside the egg
it feeds on the yolk and
grows until it is ready to hatch.

Nature

Why do owls have big eyes?

Owls have big eyes so that
they can see clearly in the dark.
All birds that hunt small animals
need good eyesight.
They must be able to detect
the slightest movements
on the ground below them.
For owls it is even harder.
They hunt by night so they need
to be able to see in the dark.
They have huge eyes that can
take in as much light as possible.
Owls can turn their heads around
so they can look behind them.
At night, owls can see up to
100 times better than people!

Why do leopards have spots?

Leopards have spots to make it
difficult for them to be seen.
Their spots help them to hide
amongst the leaves and shadows
of the forests where they live.
The leopard's spots are part
of its camouflage or disguise.
Camouflage helps hunting animals
to creep up on their victims
without being seen.
Leopards live in Africa and Asia
and they hunt by night
creeping through the jungle and
climbing trees.

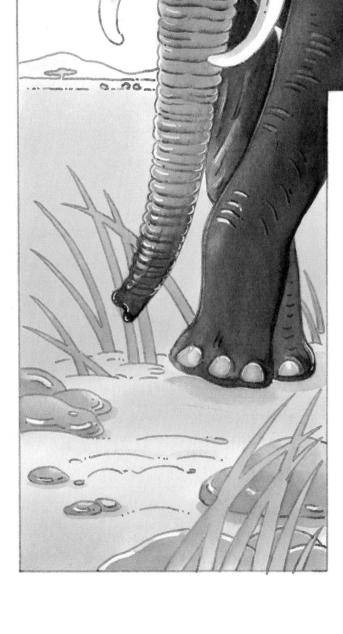

Why do elephants have big ears?

An elephant's big ears help it
to keep cool.
Some elephants live in Africa
where the sun is very hot.
To stay cool their bodies
need to be able to lose heat.
They lose heat from their blood
by passing blood through
their large ears.
They also cool down by flapping
their ears to fan themselves.
They also stick out their ears
to make themselves look fierce
when they charge an enemy.
Not all elephants have big ears.
The Indian elephant, which lives in
shady forests, has quite small ears.

Nature

How does a caterpillar turn into a butterfly?

A caterpillar turns into a butterfly by transforming itself inside a hard case called a chrysalis. Before they do this caterpillars eat many leaves and soon become fat and too big for their skin. They grow a new skin and lose their old one and this happens about five times. Then they find a quiet spot and the chrysalis forms around them. Inside the chrysalis they turn into a butterfly. After about a month the chrysalis breaks open and out comes a beautiful butterfly.

Why do butterflies have patterns on their wings?

Some butterflies have patterns on their wings to help them protect themselves and hide from enemies. Many butterflies, such as the Peacock Butterfly, have round marks on their wings which look like eyes. That is just what they are meant to look like. When a butterfly opens its wings its enemies are frightened. The enemies suddenly seem to be staring into the eyes of a terrible monster! Because its enemies are afraid the butterfly has time to escape.

Why do bees sting?

Bees will only sting people
to frighten them away
if they come too close to their hive
or if they tread on them.
Sometimes bees and other insects
sting to attack or kill creatures
for food.
Many insects can make poison
in their bodies which they use
when they sting.
A honeybee uses 22 muscles
when it stings and it often dies
in the process.

What do worms eat?

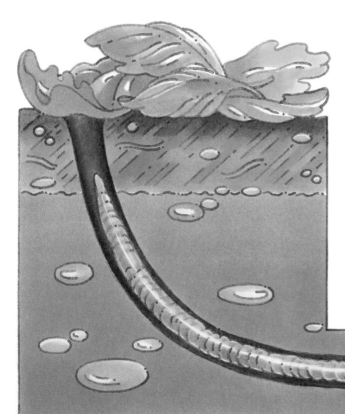

As a worm burrows in the ground
it swallows the soil.
In the soil there are tiny pieces
of rotting plants and germs.
These are the worm's food.
Anything the worm cannot use
is passed out at the other end.
Earthworms do a useful job.
They break up the soil and
fill it with air holes.
This makes it easier
for plants to grow.

Nature

Which animal can run the fastest?

The cheetah can run faster
than any other land animal.
They are big cats with
spotted coats and most of them live
in the wild in Africa.
They can race after their victims
at speeds of up to 100 km an hour.

That is about 60 miles an hour.
Even the fastest man in the
world could not run
half as fast as
a cheetah.
The athlete's world record
is about 40 km
(25 miles) an hour!
How fast can you run?

Which animal lives the longest?

There is a shellfish called
the ocean quahog that can live
to be over 200 years old!
Tortoises have been known to live
for about 150 years and
some birds and fishes have reached
80 years or more.

Which animal can jump the highest?

Kangaroos are the champions
of the high jump.
They can jump 3 m (10 ft).
However, fleas can leap as high
as about 20 cm (8 in).
That may not seem very high
but remember how tiny fleas are.
It is the same as you jumping
260 m (853 ft)!

Why do kangaroos carry their babies in pouches?

A kangaroo carries its baby in its
pouch because the baby is too small
and weak to start life alone.
A baby kangaroo, or joey,
is born long before it is ready
to look after itself.
It has to crawl into a pouch on its
mother's stomach until it is bigger.
In the pouch it feeds on its mother's
milk and is kept safe and warm.
When it is big enough it leaves
the pouch for the outside world.
There are other animals,
such as wallabies and koalas,
who carry their babies in pouches.

Nature

Can parrots really talk?

Parrots cannot really talk because they do not understand what they are saying.
But they are good at copying the noises they hear.
Parrots can copy words and whole sentences that they hear people saying.

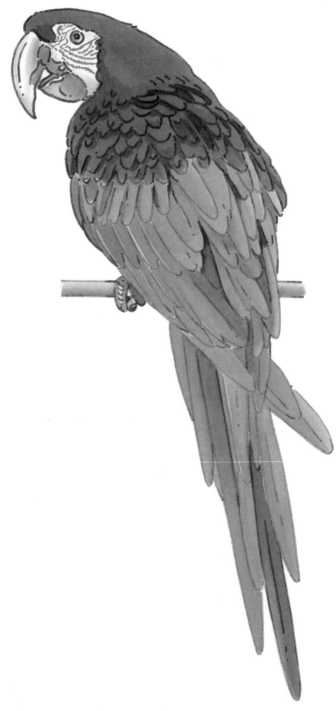

Can chimpanzees talk?

Chimpanzees cannot talk, at least not in the way we can.
But scientists have studied chimpanzees and have found that they do communicate.
They send each other all kinds of messages, using their hands and faces to make signs.
Some scientists have learned to exchange signs with chimpanzees.
No animals can talk as we do.
But many creatures can make noises or signals.
Sometimes these are used to warn other animals of danger.
Sometimes they are made to frighten away another creature or to let other animals in the group know where they are.

Are bats blind?

Bats are not actually blind, but
they do have very poor eyesight.
Very short-sighted people
sometimes describe themselves
as being blind as a bat.
Bats hunt at night and
even though it is dark
they still find insects easily and
they never bump into anything.
There is a reason for this.
When bats fly, they make a sound
which is too high for you to hear.
It bounces back off objects.
The bats can hear the sound
echoing back to them and
that is how they can find
their way around.
You can find out more about
echoes on page 108.

Why do spiders spin webs?

Spiders spin webs to catch flies and
other small insects.
Spiders' webs can look beautiful.
You can see the fine network of silk
well when dew has fallen.
But spiders' webs are really
deadly traps.
Different kinds of spiders
make different sorts of webs.
Some spin circles of thread
on spokes around the centre.
Other spiders weave nets,
hammocks or trapdoors.
The spider makes the thread
in its spinneret.
The thread begins as a sticky liquid
which dries into a silken thread.
Not all spiders spin webs.
Some hunt their prey
instead of trapping it.

Nature

How do tadpoles turn into frogs?

Tadpoles go through many changes
before they turn into frogs.
When they hatch, tadpoles look
much more like fish than frogs.
They breathe like fish
through their gills.
Gills are openings in their sides
which take in oxygen
from the water.
But after a couple of months
the tadpoles start to change.
Their gills disappear.
The tadpoles grow lungs and
are soon breathing air
from the surface of the water.
They grow back legs, then front
legs and finally their tails disappear.
After three months they look like
real frogs and are ready to hop on
to the bank.

Why do frogs jump?

Frogs use their strong legs to escape
from hungry birds or snakes.
Frogs can jump huge distances.
One kind of frog from
southern Africa has been known
to cover over 9 m (29 ft) in just
three jumps!

Why do flies buzz?

It is the sound of the fly's wings moving up and down very fast which makes the buzzing sound you hear.

This buzzing sound is made even louder because the wing muscles shake the central part of the fly's body. The shaking pushes air through breathing holes in the fly's body.

Nature

Where do squirrels go in winter?

In winter, when it gets cold,
squirrels spend a lot of time asleep
in their warm nests.
As winter approaches, squirrels hide
piles of food in holes and
hollow trees.
They can use this store of food
during the cold winter months.
On fine days they scamper out and
search for their stores of food.

Why do rabbits have long ears?

Rabbits have long ears so that
they can hear the slightest sounds.
Rabbits are gentle creatures and
they are easy to catch.
So they must always be careful.
They have many enemies such as
foxes, birds of prey, weasels,
stoats and pet dogs and cats.
A rabbit's eyes are set well back
on the sides of its head so that
it can see over a wide area.
Its long ears help it to hear clearly
and if in danger the rabbit can run.
Its white tail is a warning signal
to other rabbits telling them
that danger is near.

What is the difference between a hare and a rabbit?

There are in fact many differences
between a hare and a rabbit.
Hares are larger than rabbits.
They have longer ears, and
bigger and stronger back legs.
Rabbits live together in
underground burrows but hares
live on their own and
do not dig underground.
Instead they press down
a patch of grass with their bodies.
This is called a form and it is
where they hide their young.

Nature

How do fish breathe?

Most fish do not have lungs
so they have to take oxygen
straight from the water.
Fish take in water
through their mouths as they swim.
They squirt water out through gills
which are openings
behind the head.
The gills take in oxygen
from the water and pass it
into the fish's blood.

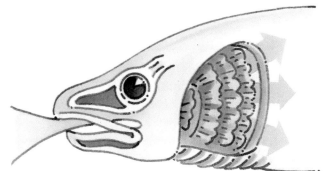

Nature

Why do crabs have shells?

Crabs have shells to protect
their soft bodies.
As they grow bigger
they have to shed their shells and
grow new ones.
This happens several times.
The hermit crab does not have
a shell of its own.
It squeezes the soft part of its body
into the shell of a whelk or winkle
and carries it around with it.

Which is the biggest animal in the world?

The blue whale is
the biggest animal in the world.
It can be over 30 m (100 ft) long
and can weigh 125 tonnes or more!
Whales are not fish but mammals
like dogs and horses.
Being a mammal means that the
mother whale gives birth to babies
and does not lay eggs and
that she feeds them on her milk.
Whales breathe air from
the surface of the water and then
dive below the waves.
They eat over a tonne of food a day!

Nature

Which is the largest bird in the world?

The largest bird in the world
is the ostrich.
It lives in Africa and can grow
to over 2.7 m (9 ft) high.
Ostriches cannot fly but
they can run quickly.
Ostriches lay very large eggs.
The eggs weigh about 1.7 kg (4 lbs)
and they are 24 times as heavy
as a hen's egg!

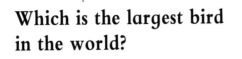

50

What is the difference between a pony and a horse?

Sometimes people think a pony is a young horse.
But a pony is a small breed or family of horse.
The shire horse (1) is very large.
The shetland pony (2) is very small.

Horses and ponies are usually measured in hands which are units of 10 cm (about 4 in).
A pony is any kind of horse which is less than 14 hands high.

1

2

Why do snakes bite?

Dangerous snakes will only bite someone in self-defence or if they are trodden on by accident.
Many people are afraid of snakes.
But most snakes are harmless.
Dangerous snakes have poison at the back of their jaws.
This poison passes through their fangs.
When the jaw is opened wide poison is forced into the fangs.
As the snake bites its enemy it injects the poison.

All about
far-away places

Far-away places

Which is the biggest country in the world?

Russia is the biggest country
in the world.
It is nearly 9000 km (5600 miles)
from east to west and
nearly 4500 km (2800 miles)
from north to south.
It is so huge that when the sun
is setting in Moscow it is rising
at the other end of the country
on its eastern coast!

Which is the biggest city in the world?

The biggest city is really two cities
which have joined together.
These are Tokyo and Yokohama.
Tokyo is Japan's capital city.
Yokohama lies south of Tokyo.
These two cities have grown so big
that they have spread together.
There are over 29 000 000 people
living in this area!
The biggest single city in the world
is Mexico City, which is
the capital of Mexico.
Over 18 000 000 people
live in and around it.

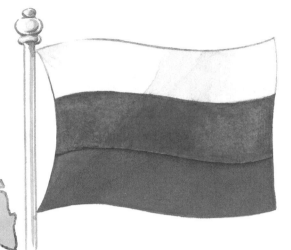

Since the country is so large
there are different climates or
weather conditions.
In the north the land is covered
with ice and snow.
In the middle there are pine forests
and wide grassy plains and hills.
In the south there are deserts and
high mountains.

Which country has the most people living in it?

China is the country with
the most people living in it.
We know this because of a census.
A census is when people count how
many are living in a country.
China has about 1 072 000 000
people living in it, which is far
more than any other country.

Far-away places

Which is the smallest country in the world?

The Vatican City State is
the smallest country in the world.
It is less than half a square km
(one fifth of a square mile)!
This is where the Pope lives
and he is the head of the
Roman Catholic Church.
The buildings where the Pope lives
are called the Vatican.
The area around the Vatican
is a real country even though
it is so small.
The Vatican is surrounded
by the city of Rome which
is the capital city of Italy.

Why do people in different countries speak different languages?

The reason why people in different
countries speak different languages
goes right back to the earliest times.
The first human beings probably
spoke to each other by grunting
and using signs.
Over thousands of years
these noises became words and
a language developed.
Where different groups met, people
began to use the same language.
But many groups of people
did not meet each other.
Because of this, different languages
developed in different parts
of the world.

Why do countries have flags?

Flags are really a sort of badge. They are used on buildings or ships to show which country owns them. Flags can also have special meanings. There are over 170 countries in the world and they all have flags. The Union Flag of Great Britain combines three different flags (1). It is made up of the flags of St Andrew (for Scotland), St George (for England) and St Patrick (for Ireland).

The flag of the United States is called the Stars and Stripes (2). It has 13 red and white stripes, one for each of the first States to join the United States of America. It has a star for each of the 50 States that make up the United States today. The flag of Germany has three horizontal stripes of black, red and gold (3).

Far-away places

Which is the highest mountain in the world?

The highest mountain is
Mount Everest, which is
8848 m (29 000 ft) above sea level.
It is part of a great chain of snowy
mountains that stretch along
the southern border of China.
They are called the Himalayas.
The first climbers to reach the
summit of Everest were Hillary and
Tenzing in 1953.

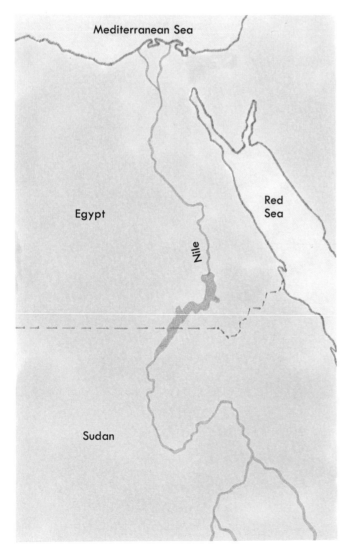

Which is the longest river in the world?

The longest river in the world
is usually thought to be the Nile.
It flows north from central Africa
and passes through Sudan and
Egypt on its way to the
Mediterranean Sea and it is about
6670 km (4144 miles) long.
Measuring exactly how long
a river is can be difficult.
Rivers are often made up
of smaller rivers and streams.
The waters split up, join together
and get lost in lakes and marshes.
The River Amazon which flows
through the forests of South
America, is a little shorter than
the Nile.
It is about 6448 km (4007 miles) long.

What are jungles?

Jungles are really rain forests.
These are thick tangles of trees,
vines and other plants which grow
in places where it rains a lot.
There are some rain forests in
the cooler parts of the world
but most rain forests grow
in very hot, damp countries.
There are many in Asia and central
Africa and a large rain forest
grows around the River Amazon
in South America.
Rain forests are full of insects and
all kinds of other animals.
There are snakes and monkeys and
brightly coloured birds.
Tigers live in the jungles of India
and jaguars live in the jungles of
South America.

Far-away places

Where is the coldest place in the world?

The coldest temperature recorded was in Antarctica: $-57°C$ ($-70°F$)! Nobody lives in Antarctica because it is too cold.
But many scientists visit Antarctica to study its rocks and weather. They also study the penguins and seals which live around the coast.

Where is the hottest place in the world?

The deserts of North Africa are among the hottest places in the world. The highest temperature recorded was in Libya: $55°C$ ($137°F$)!
In areas which are this hot, few plants can grow because there is not enough water.
People living in North Africa dress in loose robes and wear cloth around their heads to stay cool.

What is an oasis?

An oasis is a place in a desert
where you can find water.
The water comes to the surface
in a spring or from a well
which has been dug.
An oasis often has many plants.
People travelling across the desert
can stop to rest at an oasis.
They can get water for themselves
and their animals and find
shade and food.
Deserts are dry places where
there is little or no rain.
Some deserts are cold and
others are very hot.
There are few plants except
thorn bushes and cacti.

All about
the earth
and sky

The earth and sky

Why does the moon change shape?

The shape of the moon
doesn't really change,
it just looks as if it does.
This is because part of the moon
is sometimes in shadow and so
you cannot see it all
from earth.
The moon is a small planet which
travels around the earth
once a month.
At some points on this journey
the earth blocks out part of
the sun's light from the moon.
The earth's shadow falls on the
moon and so only part of the moon
is lit up.
Sometimes we see a whole circle
which we call a full moon (1).
Other times we see half a circle
which we call a half moon (2).
And sometimes we see only
a thin curve which we call
a crescent moon (3).

Why does the moon shine at night?

The moon shines at night because
it acts as a giant mirror and
reflects the light from the sun.
It doesn't actually give out
light of its own.
The moon shines not only at night,
it shines during the day as well!
The glare from the sun is so bright
during the day that you often
cannot see the moon.
But the moon is still there.

Could you live on the moon?

People cannot live on the moon because there is no water or air.
You need air and water to stay alive.
The moon is a rocky place and there are no living things.
The days are very hot and the nights are very cold.
People could only live on the moon if special bases were built with everything they needed to stay alive.

The earth and sky

Why does the sun shine?

The sun shines because
it is a huge burning ball of gas
which gives out light and heat.
The sun is really a star.
It seems to shine much brighter
than other stars because it is nearer
to the earth.
Just like the other stars you see
the sun is a ball of blazing gases
which flare and spurt flames
out into space.
The rays of light from the sun
travel through space very fast –
at about 300 000 km (186 500 miles)
per second!
And it only takes about 8 minutes
for a light ray to reach the earth
from the sun.

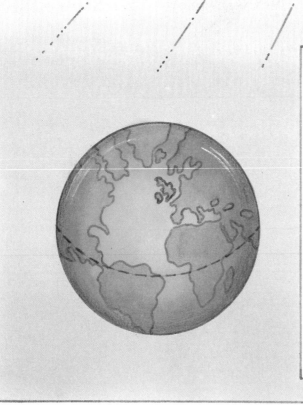

Why are some countries hotter than others?

Some countries are hotter
because they are nearer the sun.
Lands around the middle
of the earth, or equator, are
very hot because the sun's rays
have less distance to travel.
The lands which lie around the
North and South Poles are
very cold because the sun's rays
have further to travel.

Will the sun shine forever?

No, the sun cannot shine forever.
The sun is about half-way
through its life.
Eventually it will die.
It will swell up into a huge red ball
of gas and the heat may destroy
the planets around it.

Why are sunsets red?

The sun looks red when it sets
because its rays pass through
a thicker layer of air and dust.
At the start of the day
the sun rises in the east.
It then seems to move across
the sky and reaches its highest point
in the middle of the day.
In the evening it sets in the west.
But the sun is not really moving.
It is the earth which is spinning.
When the sun sets, it means that
our part of the world is turning
away from the sun's light.

The earth and sky

What are clouds?

Clouds are made of tiny drops
of water which float in the air.
They are a bit like the steam
from a boiling kettle.
When water boils in a kettle,
you see steam rising.
We say that the water is
evaporating, or being turned
into a gas.
This gas is called water vapour.
When water vapour leaves the
surface of the boiling water it rises,
cools and thickens, forming tiny
drops of water.
This is how clouds are formed.
The sun's heat evaporates water
in lakes, rivers and seas and
the water vapour rises.
As it gets higher up, it cools and
turns back into tiny drops of water.
The drops of water form clouds.

Where does rain come from?

Rain comes from clouds.
Clouds are made of millions
of little drops of water
which float in the air.
The tiny drops of water collect
together in the sky and form
the shapes we call clouds.
When it gets colder,
the tiny drops of water join up
to form larger drops.
These are too heavy to float
in the air and they fall as rain.

The earth and sky

Why are clouds different shapes?

Clouds are different shapes because they are formed in different ways. Different kinds of clouds are found at different heights and temperatures.
Some form during storms or high winds.
Others bring fine weather.
The three main groups of clouds are called cirrus, cumulus and stratus.
Cirrus clouds are wispy (1).
Cumulus clouds are puffy and they often bring rain (2).
Stratus clouds also bring rain (3).
They form blankets of cloud, often very close to the surface of the earth.

What would happen if it never rained?

If it never rained there would be no rivers, lakes or seas and the earth would become a rocky desert.
No plants would grow and animals and people could not live because there would be no water to drink.

The earth and sky

What is snow made of?

Snow is made of ice crystals
which have joined together.
When it is very cold rain freezes
in clouds to form ice crystals which
join together as white flakes.
They float to the ground as snow.
Every snowflake looks like
a six-pointed star and
each one is different.

Where does dew come from?

Dew comes from the water drops
which are in warm air (see page 68).
At night, as the earth cools down,
water vapour in the air turns back
into small drops of water.
You can see drops of dew on grass
in the early morning.

What is fog?

Fog is really a cloud that is near the ground.

A cloud is made of millions of little drops of water (see page 68).

You can see tiny drops of water on your clothes if you go for a walk when it is foggy.

Sometimes fog is so thick that you cannot see very far in front of you.

What is smog?

Smog is a mixture of smoke and fog.

When it is foggy the smoke from chimneys and the exhaust fumes from cars don't get blown away by the wind.

Instead they stay in the air and make the fog even thicker.

This is called smog.

The earth and sky

Where do rivers come from?

Most rivers come from springs.
When it rains some of the water
soaks into the earth.
It soaks through soft rocks but
it is trapped by hard rocks and this
makes underground lakes.
Water then bubbles up out of
the ground in some places.
The places where water comes out
of the ground are called springs.
Springs are where many rivers start.

As the trickle of water
from the spring flows along,
more rain water drains into it
from higher ground.
It gets bigger and bigger, becoming
a stream and then a river.
This is joined by other rivers, until
in the end there is just one large river,
flowing to the sea.

Why are there waves on the sea?

Waves are caused by wind blowing
on the surface of the sea.
You can make your own waves if
you blow across the surface
of some water in a bowl.
Gales at sea can make waves
over 30 m (100 ft) high!
Even bigger waves can be made
by earthquakes or volcanoes
under the sea.
These can be over 80 m (265 ft) tall.
They can sink ships and flood land.

Why does the wind blow?

Wind is caused when air
is at different temperatures
in different places.
On a warm day the sun
heats up the land.
The hot land heats the air above it.
The warm air (1) rises because
it expands and becomes lighter
than the cold air around it.
Cooler, heavier air then rushes in
to take its place (2).
These movements of cooler air
are what we call wind.

The earth and sky

Why shouldn't you look at the sun?

If you looked at the sun
without protecting your eyes
you would damage your eyesight.
Even though the sun is far away
from the earth, its rays
are still very strong.
Even astronomers never look
at the sun with a telescope.
They use cameras and computers
to take pictures of the sun for them
or else they look at the way the sun
is reflected on to a card.
If you did look at the sun through
a telescope its rays would blind you.

Why does thunder follow lightning?

You see a flash of lightning
the moment is strikes because
light travels faster than sound.
You hear the thunder afterwards
because you see what happens
before you actually hear it.
Lightning is really a big spark
of electricity.
It is made when drops of water
in storm clouds rub together.
Sparks of electricity flash to other
clouds or to the ground.
Lightning is hot and it heats up
the air around it.
The air gets so hot so fast that,
just like an explosion, there is
a bang which is the thunder.
If you want to know how far
away a thunder storm is, count
the number of seconds between
the lightning and the thunder.
For every three seconds
you will know it is one km away
(five seconds for one mile).

What are hailstones made of?

Hailstones are drops of water
which have turned to ice.
Hailstones form when the drops
move up to the colder part
of a cloud (the top) and freeze.
When they fall to the warmer base
of the cloud they collect other drops
of water and grow.
Eventually the hailstones become
so large and heavy that they fall
out of the cloud to the ground.

The earth and sky

Why do stars twinkle?

Stars do not actually twinkle –
it only seems as if they do.
When you look at the stars
the gases and specks of dust
that form the air around the earth
get in the way.
They stop you seeing clearly.
You can see stars much better
from the top of a mountain,
where there is less dust in the air.
But the best view is from space
where there is no air or dust and
stars do not twinkle at all.

What is a shooting star?

A shooting star is a piece of rock
flying through space which burns up
when it hits the layer of air
surrounding the earth.
This leaves a light streaking
through the sky.
Some people think shooting stars
are lucky and make wishes
whenever they see one.

Why do astronauts have to wear special suits?

Astronauts have to wear special spacesuits to protect them and keep them alive in space.
In space there are harmful rays.
It can be hot and
there is no oxygen to breathe.
A spacesuit keeps the astronaut in an atmosphere which is like the one on earth.
The suit is made of many layers.
Next to the astronaut's skin there is a water-cooled suit to keep them cool.
Over this is a tough pressure suit with oxygen inside it.
On the outside is a thick suit and helmet to protect the astronauts from rays and flying particles.

All about
long ago

Long ago

How do we know about dinosaurs?

We know that dinosaurs existed
because their fossils
have been found in rock.
Fossils are the remains
of animals or plants
which have left their mark
in rock or have actually turned
into rock themselves.
This is how it happened.
When dinosaurs died, their flesh
usually rotted away and
only the bony parts of their bodies
were left behind.
The bones became covered
with sand and mud.
Later this soil pressed together
until it became hard rock.
Sometimes the bones washed away
and their shape stayed in the rock.
Other times the bones themselves
became rock.
Scientists studied these fossils and
worked out what the dinosaurs
must have looked like and
how they lived.

What were baby dinosaurs like?

Baby dinosaurs hatched from eggs.
The eggs could be up to 30 cm (1 ft)
long and there might be
30 eggs in one batch!
When the baby dinosaurs hatched
they were very small.
They probably had to sit in the sun
to keep warm or hide in the shade
to cool down.

Long ago

Were dinosaurs fierce?

Not all dinosaurs were fierce.
Some of the largest dinosaurs were
gentle creatures who ate plants.
Smaller armour-plated dinosaurs
like Stegosaurus
were not hunters but they needed their
armour to defend themselves (1).
Apatosaurus (2) was about 20 m
(70 ft) long, and could rear up to
crop the vegetation.
Allosaurus (3) 12 m (39 ft) long was
a fierce predator.

Long ago

Why aren't there dinosaurs now?

The dinosaurs ruled the earth
for about 130 million years and
then they disappeared.
No one is sure why.
Some people think they died out
because the climate got colder.
Dinosaurs had no fur or feathers
so they probably couldn't survive
in a colder world.
The kinds of plants that grew also
changed.
Perhaps plant-eating dinosaurs
could not find the right plants to
eat and they starved to death.
Once they died out then
the meat-eating dinosaurs
would also have died because
they would not have any food.
Some people think dinosaurs died
because a large rock from space
hit the earth at a great speed
killing the dinosaurs.

What did the first people look like?

The first people would have looked
rather like the apes of today.
They were shorter than we are and
had low, sloping foreheads (1).
The first people to look like us
lived over 25 000 years ago called
Cro-Magnon Man (2).

Did people really live in caves?

Yes, long ago before people
learned to build huts
they found that caves
made very good homes.
Caves were safe from wild animals
and could be easily defended
against enemies.
Caves offered shelter from the wind
and rain and could be made
quite warm with a fire.
In some parts of the world
people still live in caves.

Long ago

What were the first clothes like?

The first clothes were
animal skins and furs.
People cut them up and stitched
them together with strips of skin (1).
They softened the animal skins by
beating or even chewing it.
They made the skins water-proof
by soaking them in a mixture
of water and bark from trees.
This is called tanning.

Soon people began to use goat hair
and sheep's wool for warm clothes.
Wool could be soaked and beaten
until it turned into felt.
It could also be spun into thread
and then woven into cloth (2).
Plants like cotton could also
be spun and woven.
The cloth was cut and stitched
to make simple tunics (3).

Why did people build castles?

People built castles
to defend themselves
from their enemies.
People living in castles could hide
behind the walls and fight off
their enemies.
They could shoot arrows or
throw rocks at their attackers.
Their enemies would try to knock
down the castle walls.
Often they would wait
outside the castle until
the soldiers inside ran out of food
and gave themselves up.
The first castles were hill forts,
which were built on the tops of hills
with big ditches dug around them.
Later castles were built of stone and
surrounded by thick walls.

Long ago

Who invented the alphabet?

There is not just one alphabet.
There are 65 different alphabets
used in the world today!
We do not know who invented
the first alphabet.
But the earliest alphabet
we know about was used
nearly 3500 years ago in Syria
made up of little lines which had
been pressed into clay tablets.
Our own alphabet is based on the
one used by the Romans (right).

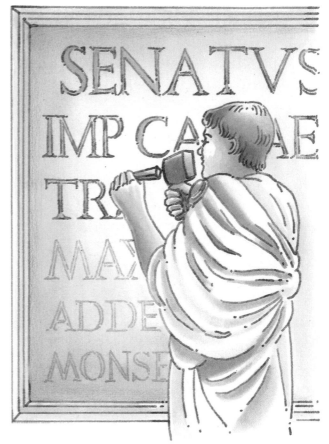

Have people always used money?

People have not always used
money because long ago
they did not need to buy things.
People hunted animals for food or
gathered fruit and berries.
When people learned to farm and
to make things, they swapped these
for tools or other useful objects
instead of using money.
But they soon found it easier to use
metal tokens to pay for things.
These were the first coins.
Coins were easy to carry and
the metal was worth the same
wherever people traded.
Metal was also easy to weigh and
coins were often stamped with
a picture to show how much
they were really worth.

Did children go to school long ago?

Long ago children did not go to school, at least not to the types of schools we have today.
They were taught to fight in battles and shown how to use swords and bows and arrows.
They learned how to spin and weave and how to farm the land.
Some children were taught to work at a craft or trade and
they were called apprentices.
Monks and priests taught a few children to read and write.

Long ago

What toys did children have long ago?

The first toys were very simple such as dolls, skittles or hoops which could be rolled along the ground. Children in ancient Egypt played with toy tigers made from bronze. About 500 years ago, children were playing with toy soldiers and horses and tiny pots and pans made of clay.
The best-loved toy of all was the teddy bear.
Teddy bears were first made in the United States and Germany about 90 years ago.
They were named after the American President, Theodore Roosevelt, whose nickname was Teddy.
The President used to hunt for bears and one day he found a lost bear cub.
A cartoon of the time showed Teddy with the little bear.

Long ago

What are Christmas trees for?

People use Christmas trees for decoration and also to remind them of the first Christmas.
In the cold northern parts of the world people have always liked to decorate their homes in the middle of winter.
Christmas trees, or firs, can make rooms look cheerful when it is snowy outside and many branches are bare.
Fir trees were first brought inside at Christmas in Germany.
They were covered in candles and hung with presents.
Over 100 years ago, people in other countries started having Christmas trees.
A star was put on top of the tree to remind people of the star that led the shepherds to Jesus.

Long ago

What were the first bicycles like?

The first bicycle did not have
any brakes or pedals.
Riders sat on the saddle and pushed
the machine along with their legs.
The first bicycle with pedals was
invented by a Scottish man called
Kirkpatrick Macmillan in 1839.
Some early bicycles were called
penny-farthings (1).
At that time a British penny was
a very large coin, and a farthing
was a very small one.
The penny farthing had a huge
front wheel and a tiny back one!
About 100 years ago the bicycles
we use first became popular (2).

What were the first cars like?

The first car was more like
a tractor than a car and
it was powered by steam (3).
The first real cars were built
in Germany about 100 years ago
by a man called Karl Benz (4).
They had thin wheels like bicycles
and were driven by petrol.

90

Long ago

What were the first aeroplanes like?

The first aeroplanes were gliders.
They were pulled along on a rope
and flew like kites (1).
In 1903, two American brothers
called Orville and Wilbur Wright
managed to fly a real plane (2).
It had a fuel engine which drove
two propellers.
The propellers were fixed behind
two sets of wings.
Planes with two sets of wings
are called bi-planes.
These early planes were very light
and they could only fly
very slowly.

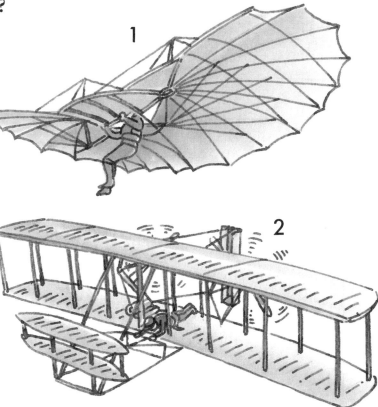

Who sailed around the world first?

There were in fact several people
who were first to sail
around the world.
They were the Spanish crew
of Ferdinand Magellan,
who was a sea captain
working for the King of Spain.
In 1519 Magellan left Spain
with five ships to cross
the Atlantic Ocean.
He found a narrow sea passage
through South America
which is today named the
Strait of Magellan after him.
He sailed across the Pacific Ocean
but he was killed by warriors
in the Philippine Islands.
His crew sailed on,
passed South Africa and
returned to Spain in 1522.

All about
how things work

How things work

Why is glue sticky?

Glue is sticky because it is made up
of tiny particles, or molecules,
which link together very closely.
A molecule is a
small group of atoms.
All things are made
up of atoms.
They are the building blocks of life.
A simple sort of glue can be made
with flour and water.
Other glues can be made from
animal bones, rubber or plastics.

How do pencils work?

Inside pencils there is a
thin stick of graphite.
Graphite is made of carbon.
Carbon is black and greasy and
it leaves a mark on the paper
as you write.
The wood around the graphite
stops it from breaking and
makes it easy to hold.
Graphite pencils were invented
in 1795 by Nicholas Conté.

How do ballpoint pens work?

Inside a ballpoint pen there is
a plastic tube full of sticky ink.
At the end of the tube there is
a small ball of metal or nylon.
As you write the ball rolls around,
picks up the ink and makes marks
on the paper.
When the ball is not rolling
it seals the end of the plastic tube.
This stops the ink from drying out
and leaking.

How do rubbers rub out?

When you rub anything together
tiny pieces from one surface
swap places with tiny pieces
from the other surface.
This is what happens when
you rub out a pencil mark.
Rubbers are made of rubber or
plastic and pencil marks
are made of graphite.
Graphite is made of carbon and
it is black and greasy.
The graphite is picked up
by the surface of the rubber
which normally crumbles away
as you rub.
When you wipe away
the little pieces of dirty rubber
you are left with a clean page.

How things work

What is glass made of?

Glass is synthetic.
It is made from sand
which has been heated
with limestone and chalk.
The mixture is heated in
a type of oven called a furnace.
It is heated until it is very hot and
then it is left to cool down.
Metals are added to give the glass
certain colours.
Iron makes glass green and
copper makes it red.
As the mixture cools
it becomes gooey and can be made
into any shape.
Glass bottles are made by putting
hot glass in a mould and then
blowing air into the mould
to push the glass into shape.
Today this can be done by machines
but it used to be done by hand.

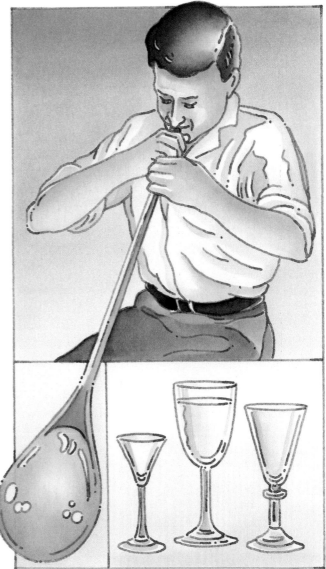

What is plastic made of?

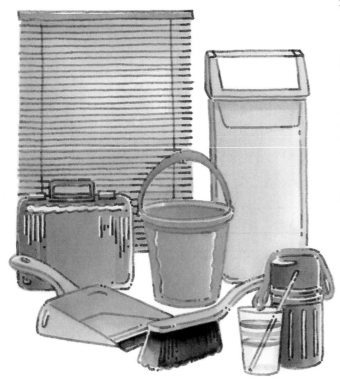

Plastic is also synthetic.
That means it does not come
from plants or animals.
Plastic is made from chemicals
which are created when oil, coal or
natural gas are heated.
There are many different kinds
of plastics.
Some are hard and some are soft.
They are used to make all kinds
of things that we use every day
like records, clothes, shoes, rope and
string, windows and tyres.

How is paper made?

Paper is mostly made from
wood chips and old rags.
These are beaten, shredded and
mixed with water or treated with
chemicals until they form a pulp.
Glue and bleach are added.
Water is removed from the pulp,
leaving a flat layer.
This layer is squeezed by big rollers
and heated so that the fibres dry
and stick together.
This produces rolls of paper
which can then be cut up
into smaller sheets.

How things work

How does water come out of the tap?

Water comes out of the tap
from pipes which take water
from reservoirs into your home.
Rainwater is collected in big lakes,
called reservoirs.
From the reservoirs the water goes
down pipes to the waterworks
where it is cleaned.
The water soaks through sand and
gravel and this filters out any dirt.
Chemicals are used to kill germs.
Then the clean water is pumped
along big pipes under roads.
The pipes take clean water
into your home.
When you turn on the tap
you open up the pipes and
the clean water comes out.

How things work

What is toothpaste made of?

Toothpaste contains fluoride and other chemicals which get rid of the layer of germs that can build up on your teeth.
This layer is known as plaque.
Plaque forms acid which eats into the hard white enamel that covers the teeth.
The fluoride in toothpaste also strengthens the enamel on your teeth and helps to keep teeth white.
Toothpaste also has a tiny amount of detergent in it which makes it go frothy when you use it.

What is soap made of?

Soap is made from animal fats, vegetable oils and soda.
Perfume is often added to give soap a pleasant smell.
Long ago soap was made from wood ash and animal fats.

How things work

Why does wool keep you warm?

Woollen jumpers are good
at keeping you warm because
they trap a layer of still air
around your body.
Heat does not easily move
through still air so this layer of
still air stops you losing heat
to the moving air around you.
Things which trap air and
keep it still are good insulators.
Sheep's wool is a good insulator
because it is curly and traps air
in the spaces especially well.
It also has grease in it and so
it keeps out water and damp too.

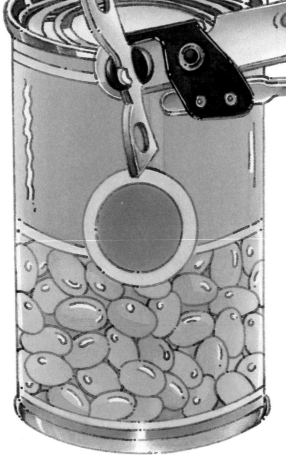

How do can-openers work?

Most can-openers have a double
lever as a handle.
On the end of one lever is
a cutting blade.
On the end of the other lever is a
wheel which is turned by a handle.
First you place the cutter blade
against the rim of the can.
Then you squeeze the levers and
turn the handle.
This pierces the can and opens it.

How does a vacuum flask work?

A vacuum flask can keep the liquid
inside it warm or cold
for several hours.
This is because there is a vacuum
between the inside and the outside
of the flask.
A vacuum is an empty space which
does not even have any air in it.
Because there is no air in a vacuum,
no heat can pass through it.
So things inside the flask remain
at the same temperature
for a long time.
Inside a flask there is a container
with double walls.
All the air is removed from between
the walls making a vacuum.
If you look inside a flask
you will see a silver-coloured glass.
This also helps to keep the heat in
because it reflects it or bounces it
back like a mirror reflecting light.

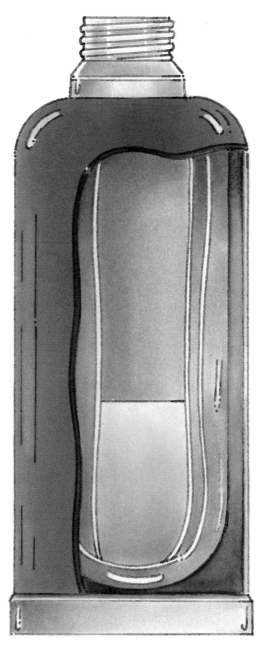

How do matches light?

Matches light because their tips
are coated with chemicals and
they are made of dry wood.
When you rub the match along
the side of the matchbox you make
the head of the match very hot.
The heat makes the chemicals
in the head of the match
burn brightly and the fire heats the
matchstick which then burns.

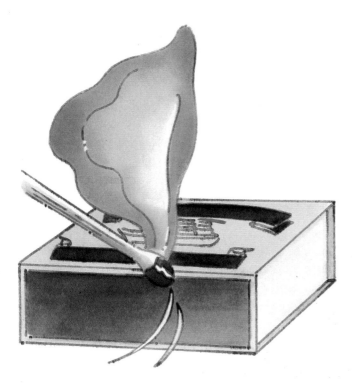

How things work

How do torches work?

Torches work by using electricity
from batteries to light up a bulb.
Inside a battery there is a rod
of carbon surrounded by
a paste of chemicals (1).
When the torch is switched on
the carbon reacts with the
chemicals to produce electricity.
The current of electricity flows
to the bulb and heats the filament.
The filament is the small wire
in the middle of a bulb (2).
The filament gets so hot that
it glows and lights up.
A mirror around the bulb reflects
the light forward so that it forms
a beam in the dark.

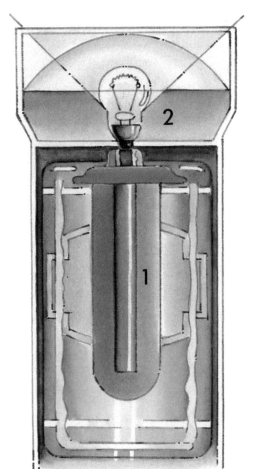

How do vacuum cleaners work?

Inside a vacuum cleaner there is a
fan powered by an electric motor.
The fan sucks in air (1).
A brush fixed to the vacuum
cleaner loosens dirt from
the surface of the carpet (2).
The dust is sucked in with the air
and trapped by a filter bag (3).
When the bag is full of dust
it can be emptied.
Before vacuum cleaners were
invented in 1901, sweeping and
cleaning carpets was
very hard work.

Why do boats float?

If you put a piece of wood in water
it floats because it is light.
But if you put an iron bar in water
it will sink.
The largest oil tankers can weigh
more than 500 000 tonnes
and yet they don't sink!
This is partly because they have
a lot of air inside them.
It is also because the force
of the water against the bottom
of the ship holds it up.

When anything enters water
it pushes some water aside.
The water then pushes back
on to the object.
You can feel this happening
if you put on rubber gloves and
put your hands under water.
It is the same with boats.
The bottom of the boat
pushes water aside.
The water then presses back
against the bottom of the boat and
pushes it up.
And so the boat floats.

How things work

How do aeroplanes fly?

Aeroplanes fly because they are
held up by a cushion of air.
It works like this.
An aeroplane has curved wings.
The curve is greater on top
of the wing than underneath.
As the engine pushes the aeroplane
forward, air is forced over and
under the wings.

But because of the shape
of the wing, air moves faster
over the top of the wing
than it does underneath it.
Fast moving air is lighter
than slower moving air.
Beneath the wing the air is moving
slower and therefore it is heavier.
So the air underneath pushes
the wing upwards and lifts
the aeroplane into the air.

Why do you put petrol in a car?

You put petrol in a car because
this is what makes it go.
Cars work by burning petrol.
The burning petrol turns the engine
and this makes the wheels move.
In a car engine the petrol
is mixed with air.
This is done in the carburettor.
The mixture makes a gas
called petrol vapour.
If a spark is fired in this mixture
it will explode.
It is this explosion which turns
the engine and makes
the car wheels move.

How do trains move?

Some trains are electric trains and
they move because they are
powered by electricity (right).
Electricity is fed to the train
along overhead wires or through
special rails beside the track.
This goes to an electric motor
in the train which turns the wheels.
Other trains are driven by
diesel engines (below).
The diesel engine drives
a generator.
This gives power for electric motors
which drive the wheels.
Trains have wheels with rims
which fit over the rail.
This holds the train on the track
and guides it as it travels along.

How things work

Why are greenhouses warm?

Why are greenhouses warm?

A greenhouse traps the sun's rays
and keeps plants warm when
the weather is cold.
The sun's rays pass through
the panes of glass and warm
the inside of the greenhouse.
The glass holds the heat in and
also protects the plants from
wind and frost.

Why do metal things feel cold?

Heat passes through metal
very easily, so we call it
a good conductor of heat.
When you touch metal the warmth
from your body passes through
the metal immediately.
This makes your fingertips feel cold.
When you touch wood
it doesn't feel cold.
This is because it does not conduct
heat well and does not carry away
the heat from your fingertips.

How do keys open doors?

Keys are cut to a special pattern
which exactly matches
its lock pattern.
If you look at a lock, you will see
that there is a metal bar going
from the door into the door frame.
The bar is held in position by a
row of pins or levers inside the lock.
The key raises the pins or levers.
The bar is then free to move and
will slide out from the slot
when you turn the key.

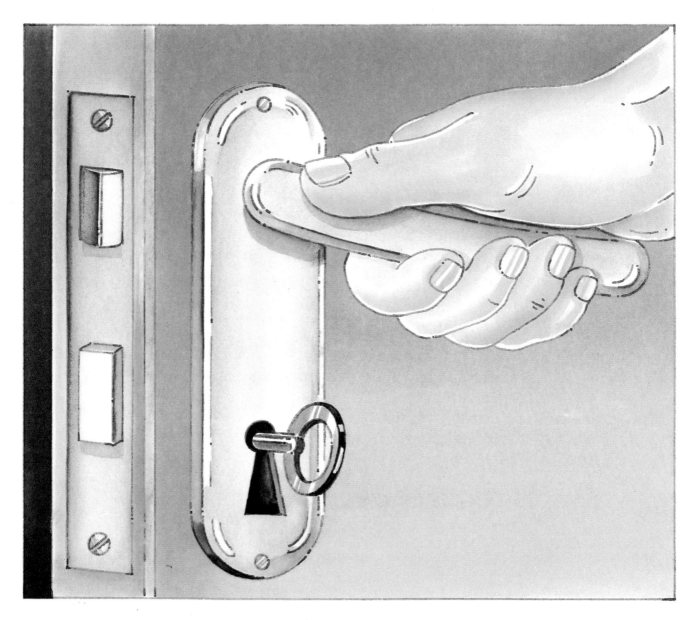

How things work

How do traffic lights work?

Some traffic lights are set to change
every few minutes.
Others are linked to a computer.
Each car sets off an electronic
signal as it nears the lights.
The signal passes from underneath
the road to the computer which
tells how busy the road is.
It can decide how often
to change the lights so that
traffic jams do not build up.

What is an echo?

An echo is a sound which bounces
off a surface and travels back
to you so that you hear it
a second time.
If you stand in front of a cliff or
a wall you may hear the sound
of your voice return as an echo.
This is because sound travels
through the air in waves.
When it strikes an object it is
bounced back again, a bit like
a ball hitting a wall.
Ships use echo sounders to work out
whether the water is deep enough
for the ship to go through.
Sounds are sent through the water
and echo back from the sea-bed.
The echoes are measured and timed
and the depth of the water
can be worked out.

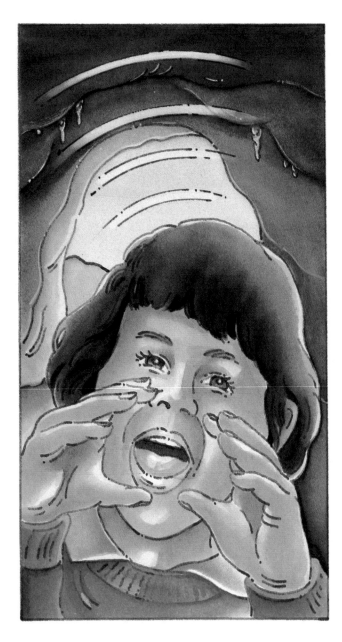

How do pianos work?

When you look at a piano
keyboard you see a row of black
and white keys.
Each of these keys is a sort of lever.
When you press it, it makes a little
hammer strike against metal strings
inside the piano.
The strings are different lengths.
Some are thicker than others so
when the hammer strikes them they
vibrate differently.
This makes different notes sound.

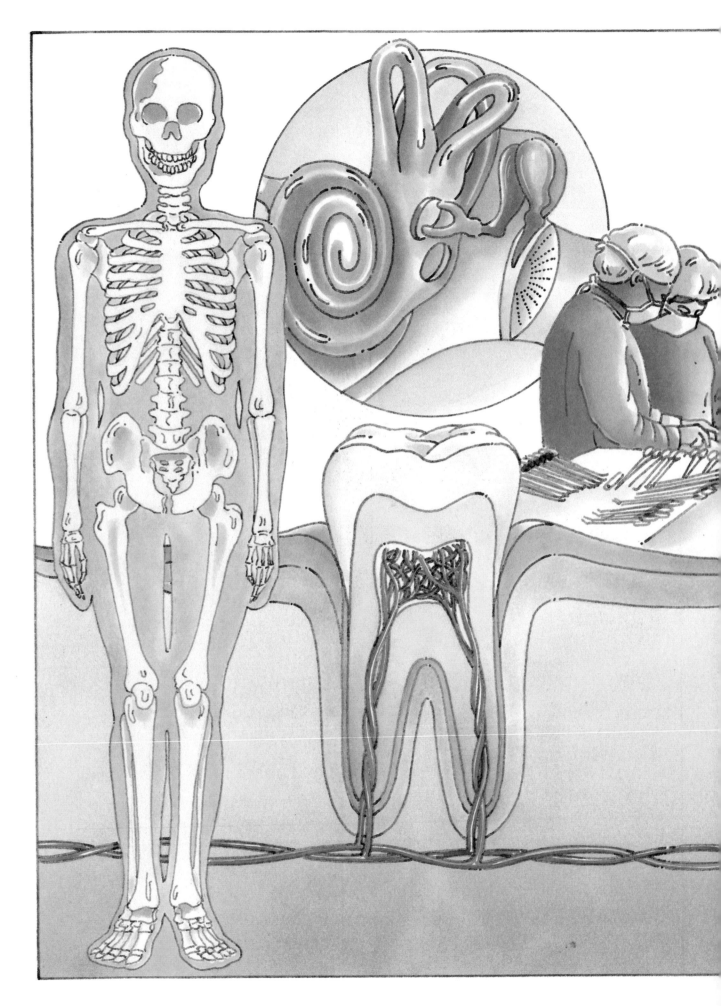

All about
ourselves

Ourselves

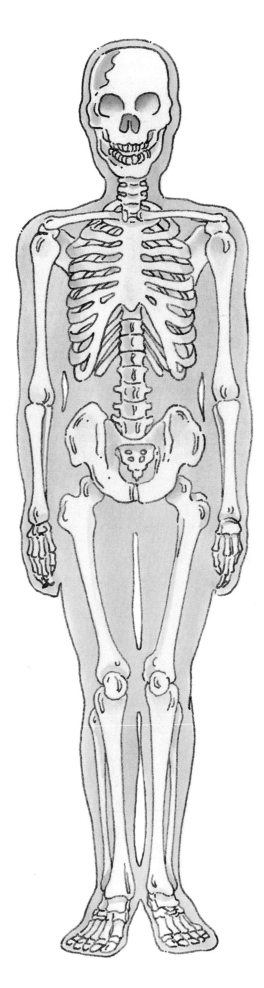

How many bones do you have?

An adult has 206 bones and a baby
has even more – about 350!
As you grow, many of these bones
join together.
The biggest bone is the femur
or thigh-bone.
The smallest bone is the stirrup
which is inside your ear.
It has that name because
it looks like a stirrup.
(Look on page 125.)
Over half your bones are in
your hands and feet!

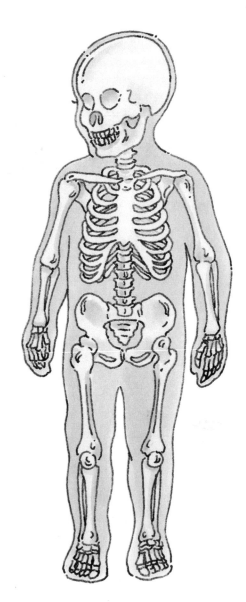

How do broken bones get better?

Broken bones get better because
bones heal themselves naturally.
Blood clots, or thickens, around
the break to protect it.
The broken ends soften and
new bone grows up between them.
When you have a broken leg
you are taken to hospital and
the doctor makes sure that the broken
parts of the bone are
lined up correctly.
Then your leg is fixed
or set in plaster until the new bone
has grown.
The plaster is then taken off.

What are bones made of?

About one third of a living bone
is made of water!
But bones are also made of cells.
Cells are the building blocks
of your body.
The outside of the bone is hard but
the inside is spongy.
Your largest bones have jelly-like
material called bone marrow
in the centre.
New blood cells are made here.

Ourselves

Why do people wear glasses?

People wear glasses
to help them to see.
Some people are short-sighted
which means they cannot see things
far away clearly.
Some people are long-sighted
which means they cannot see
close objects clearly.
Glasses can help to correct
their vision.
Rays of light enter your eye
through your pupil which is
the black spot in the middle
of your eye (1).
They focus, or meet, on the retina
which is a light-sensitive screen
at the back of your eye (2).
The retina is where the image
forms, a bit like the film
in a camera.
If the shape of the eye is not quite
right the rays do not form a sharp,
clear image on the retina and so
what you see is rather like
a photograph out of focus.
Glasses make the rays of light focus
on the right spot on the retina
so that you can see things clearly.

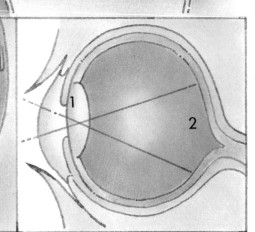

Why do people have different coloured hair?

Why is some hair curly and some hair straight?

The type of hair you have depends on the shape of the follicle it grows from.
Hair follicles are the deep holes in the skin from which hair grows.
Curly hair grows from rectangular follicles.
Wavy hair grows from oval ones.
Straight hair grows from round ones.
People often have the same kind of hair as the rest of their family.

People can have black, brown, red, yellow or white hair.
What colour your hair is depends on the amount of dark pigment, or colouring, your body makes.
This pigment is called melanin and it is made in the roots of the hair under the skin.
You often have the same hair colour as your parents or grandparents.
When people get old their hair keeps growing but their hair cells stop making melanin, so their hair turns grey and then white.

Ourselves

Why do you sometimes feel giddy?

You feel giddy sometimes because
you lose your sense of balance.
Your sense of balance is controlled
inside your ears.
Deep inside each ear there are
three little tubes full of liquid.
This liquid moves around in
the tubes as you move.
Little hairs at the end of the tubes
record the movements of the liquid
and send messages along nerves
to the brain.
These tell the brain whether
the body is properly balanced.
If you spin around and around,
you soon feel giddy because
the liquid in your ears is spinning
around too, and the messages to
your brain are all mixed up.

How do you get a suntan?

You get a suntan because your skin
is protecting itself from the sun
by becoming darker.
The dark skin of a suntan helps to
shield the tissues beneath
from the sun's harmful rays.
There are many kinds of rays
from the sun and one kind
is called ultraviolet.
Too many ultraviolet rays
can be harmful.
A small amount of ultraviolet rays
help your body to make vitamin D
which is good for the skin.

Why do people have different coloured skin?

People have different coloured skin because of the different pigment or colouring their bodies make.
This pigment is called melanin.
Darker skin gives better protection against the rays of the sun.

That is why, long ago, people who lived in sunny places came to have dark skins while people living in the cold north came to have pale skins. Today many black people live in cold countries and many white people live in hot countries.

Ourselves

Why do you brush your teeth?

You brush your teeth to keep your
mouth free of germs that can
damage your teeth.
When you eat, bits of food
stick to your teeth.
If you do not clean them, the food
can breed germs which make acid.
The acid gradually eats away
at the hard outer covering of your
tooth and can make a hole.
This gives you toothache!
The picture shows you what the
inside of a tooth looks like.
The tough outside of a tooth
is called enamel (1) and underneath
there is a softer material
called denvine (2).
In the middle of the tooth there is a
mixture of nerves and blood vessels.

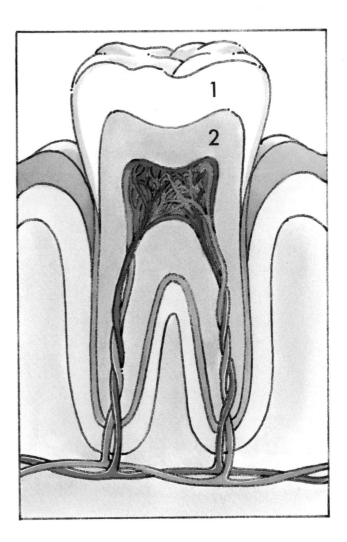

Why do your first teeth go wobbly and come out?

Your first teeth fall out to make
room for a new set of teeth
to come through.
Babies are born without any teeth.
Their first teeth begin to grow
when they start to eat solid food.
These are sometimes called milk
teeth and children have 20 of them.
As they grow their jaws grow too
so there is room for more and
bigger teeth.
The milk teeth fall out and
a new set of bigger teeth
comes through.

What are different teeth for?

Your teeth have different shapes
for different jobs.
The front teeth, called incisors,
are for cutting food (1).
The single long pointed teeth at the
corners of each jaw are called
canines and they are for tearing
food (2).
The wide teeth at the back,
called molars and premolars,
are for grinding and chewing (3).

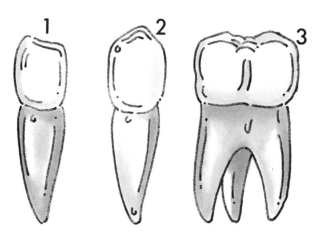

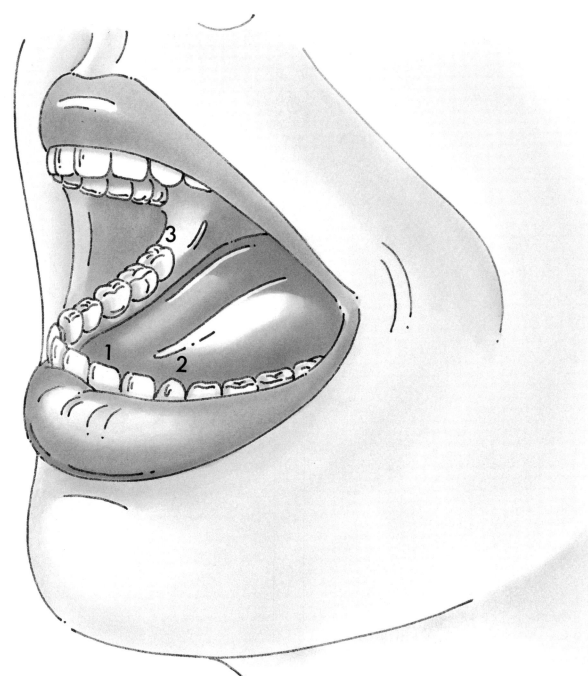

Ourselves

Why do you go to sleep?

You go to sleep to give
your body a rest so that it can
keep working properly.
Sleep gives you the chance to
build up energy for the next day.
When you are asleep
your muscles take a rest and
your heart beats slower.
Your brain keeps your body
ticking over while you sleep.

Why do you have dreams?

Scientists think that dreams
are the brain's way of sorting out
all the confusing things that have
happened to you during the day.
For part of the night
you only sleep lightly and
this is when you dream.

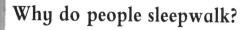

Why do people sleepwalk?

People sleepwalk when they dream
and the brain has become confused.
In dreams, the brain sometimes
finds it hard to decide whether the
person is really asleep or awake.
So it sometimes tells the body to walk.
Sleepwalkers can walk
a long way without waking up.
But don't worry — most people
are not sleepwalkers!

Ourselves

Why do babies drink milk?

Babies drink milk because
when they are first born
they do not have any teeth and
they cannot eat solid food.
Milk is full of goodness and
it has calcium in it which helps
babies to grow strong.
Some babies suck milk from
their mother's breast and some
drink milk from bottles.

Why do babies cry?

Babies cry to let us know when
they are hungry or unhappy.
Before babies learn to talk
they have to communicate
in other ways.
Crying is a good way to do this.
When their first teeth start to come
through their gums hurt and
this makes them cry.

Why do babies sleep so much?

Babies need to sleep to rest and
build up energy just as we do.
Newborn babies need twice
as much sleep as older children.
They sleep about 16 hours a day.
This is because growing up
is hard work and babies
need a lot of energy to do it!

Ourselves

Why do you get goose pimples?

You usually get goose pimples
when you are cold.
Long ago humans were hairy.
This helped them to keep warm.
People still have tiny hairs
over most of their body and these
hairs are still important in keeping
your body warm.
When you are cold, tiny muscles
in your skin raise these hairs.
The hairs trap warm air
around your body.
As the hairs rise up they make
bumps on your skin which are
called goose pimples.

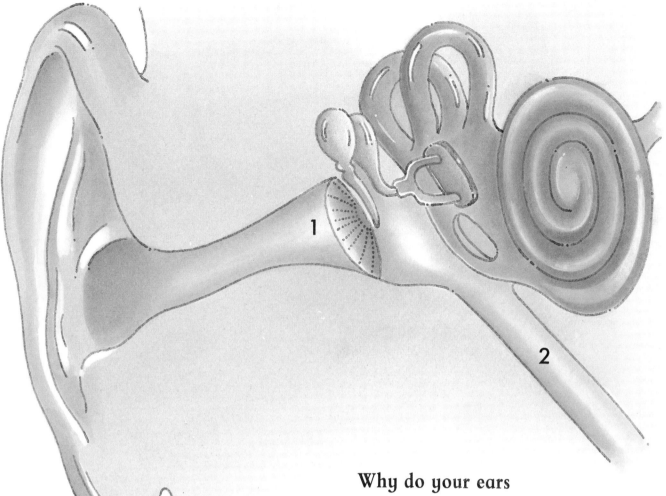

Why do your ears sometimes go pop?

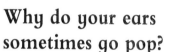

Your ears go pop when pressure
on your ears changes.
Sounds enter your ears in waves.
When they meet your eardrums
inside your ear, they make them
vibrate (1).
Your eardrums are kept tight
by air pressure from the inside.
The air comes from a tube which
links your throat to your ears (2).
When you are in a plane or
climbing a hill, the pressure
on your eardrums changes.
This makes your ears go pop.
If you swallow hard, air from your
throat will be forced up the tubes
to make them tight again.

Why do you yawn?

Yawning is your body's way
of dealing with tiredness or
lack of air.
When you yawn you take in
a great gulp of air into your lungs.
This brings in more oxygen and
helps to give you more energy.
Sometimes you yawn when
you see someone else yawning!

Ourselves

What makes you feel hungry?

If you haven't eaten for a while,
the sugars in your blood which
give you energy become used up.
Your brain detects this and
tells you to eat and this makes
you feel hungry.
When you want to eat,
your body prepares to digest food.
Saliva comes into your mouth
to help you swallow the food easily.
At the same time juices enter your
stomach to help with digestion.
You can sometimes
hear this happening when
your stomach rumbles!

What happens to the food you eat?

After you have chewed and
swallowed food, it starts
on a long journey.
It takes a day or more for food
to pass through your body and
it has to travel through 9 m (30 ft)
of digestive system!
The food travels down a tube
to your stomach.
The walls of your stomach (1)
squeeze the food and
give off juices and acid.
This makes the food safe and
breaks it down into a liquid.
The food then passes into a long tube
called the small intestine (2).
Here the goodness from the food
is sent out into the blood.
The remaining mixture then goes
into the large intestine (3).
This removes the water and
squeezes the remains into a solid
mass which is passed from your
body when you go
to the toilet.

127

Ourselves

Why do you get colds?

You get colds from tiny germs which you breathe into your body. Colds can be spread by coughing and sneezing which pass germs from one person to another. Cold germs give you watery eyes and a runny nose.

Why do you get bruises?

You get bruises if you bump into something or hit yourself. When this happens, your skin does not break but a dark patch appears. This is because tiny blood vessels beneath the skin have been crushed.

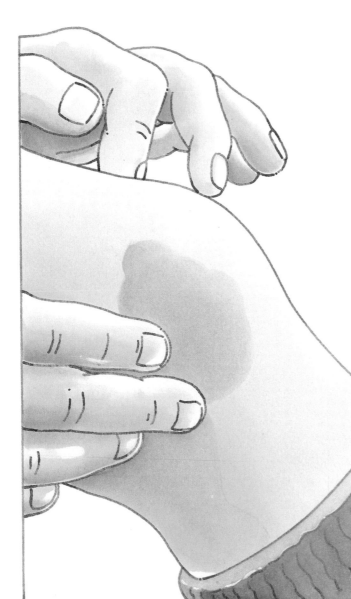